The Hudson River & the Highlands

Junction of the Hudson and Opalescent Rivers near the Headwaters, Adirondack Park

The Hudson River & the Highlands

THE PHOTOGRAPHS OF ROBERT GLENN KETCHUM

ESSAY BY JAMES THOMAS FLEXNER

AFTERWORD BY ROBERT GLENN KETCHUM

AN APERTURE BOOK

This book is dedicated to my mother and father,
Jack and Virginia Ketchum, who have supported and
encouraged me even though they often feared I
was tilting at windmills.   ROBERT GLENN KETCHUM

THE LILA ACHESON WALLACE FUND PROVIDED SUPPORT TO THE
PHOTOGRAPHER AND FOR THE PUBLICATION OF THIS BOOK.

Copyright © 1985 Aperture, a division of Silver Mountain Foundation, Inc.;
Photographs and afterword © 1985 Robert Glenn Ketchum; Essay © 1985 James
Thomas Flexner. All rights reserved under International and Pan-American
Copyright Conventions. Distributed in the United States by Viking Penguin
Inc.; in Canada by Penguin Books Canada Limited, Markham, Ontario; in the
United Kingdom and Europe, excluding France, Germany, Scandinavia and Italy,
by Phaidon Press Limited, Oxford; and in Australia by George Allen & Unwin
Australia Pty. Ltd. ISBN: 0-89381-174-2. Library of Congress Catalog Number:
85-70048. Manufactured by Editor, Italy. Book design by Wendy Byrne.

Aperture, a division of Silver Mountain Foundation, Inc., publishes a periodical,
books, and portfolios to communicate with serious photographers and creative
people everywhere. A complete catalog will be mailed upon request. Address:
20 East 23 Street, New York City, New York 10010.

TEXT CREDITS The quotes used in this text are reprinted through the kind permis-
sion of their publishers: p. 16 Boyle, Robert. *The Hudson River*. New York:
W.W. Norton & Co. Inc., 1969; p. 24 Lambert, John. *Travels Through Canada
And The United States of North America In The Years 1806, 1807, And 1808*.
London: C. Cradock And W. Joy, 1814; p. 28 Cooper, James Fenimore. *The Last
Of The Mohicans*. London: John Miller, New Bridge St., 1826; p. 28 Lossing,
Benson. *The Hudson, From The Wilderness To The Sea*. New York: Virtue and
Yorston, 1866; p. 40 Hoffman, Charles Fenno. *The New York Book of Poetry*.
New York: George Dearborn, 1837. p. 48 James, Henry. *The American Scene*.
London: Chapman and Hall, 1907; p. 56 Noble, Louis. *The Course Of Empire,
Voyage Of Life And Other Pictures Of Thomas Cole*. New York: Cornish Lam-
port & Company, 1853; p. 66 Mylod, John. *Biography Of A River: The People
and Legends of the Hudson Valley*. Edited by Alec Thomas. Copyright © 1969
by Auric Arts Film Productions, Inc. A Hawthorn Book. Reprinted by permission
of E.P. Dutton, A Division of New American Library. p. 72 Nutting, Wallace.
New York Beautiful. New York: Dodd Mead & Company, 1927; p. 80 Wolfe,
Thomas. *Of Time And The River*. New York: Charles Scribner's Sons, copyright
1935; Copyright renewed © 1963 Paul Gitlin, Administrator, C.T.A. Reprinted
with permission of Charles Scribner's Sons.

The Hudson

JAMES THOMAS FLEXNER

The Hudson is unique, unrivaled in the variety and perculiarity of its manifestations by any other river on the globe.

The Hudson rises precipitously among the northern mountains but during most of its extent it belongs both to the ocean and the land. It runs into a deep trench far under the Atlantic. However, in its now visible manifestation, its southern tidal boundary is where Sandy Hook marks off, like a parenthesis, the open ocean from the wide mouth of the Lower New York Bay. The tides advance inland through Gravesend Bay (north of Coney Island), contract into the Narrows (now spanned by the Verrazano Bridge), widen out again in the Upper Bay between Staten Island and the western shore of Long Island, pass Bedloe's Island (where the Statue of Liberty stands) and, having traveled some fifteen miles from the Atlantic, reach the lower tip of Manhattan Island. But the confrontation with one of the world's greatest cities does not stop the tides for a moment. They charge northward, up the Hudson River, passing between Manhattan and New Jersey, carrying the ocean's briny water some eighty miles inland. The pulse of the sea is felt all the way to the Hudson's upper city, Albany, some one hundred and eighty miles from the ocean and one hundred and fifty from lower Manhattan.

This deep tidal invasion of the sea is made possible by two phenomena. The Hudson drains only a restricted hinterland and amazingly is joined, during the entire trip to the ocean, by only one tributary of any dimension, the Mohawk River. On its broad trip to the sea, the Hudson fights the tides with surprisingly little water, and the river bed is almost completely lacking in the declivity that would give the river a powerful downward flow. The head of a moderately tall man standing at sea level rises as high as Albany.

Some good soul with a taste for such measurement has made the following analysis which I am glad I did not have to attempt myself. Each of the ebb tides that flow out every twenty-four hours carries driftwood a dozen miles down the Hudson, but each of the intervening flood tides propels the driftwood back two-thirds of that distance. A drop of water takes three weeks to journey from Albany to New York City.

This languor presents us with a major paradox. So gentle and oscillating a flow could cut in the softest land no more than a shallow indentation, but the Hudson Valley is such a fissure as could be carved out of a rocky terrain only by a terrific current. Clearly the valley must once have dropped much more steeply. But where did the imperious water come from? Historical geologists who spend happy careers moving mountains and continents around like chessmen, closing and opening oceans, have theory after theory. Perhaps the water that now fills the Great Lakes once drained into the Hudson.

A geologic formation which you can climb around on, if you please, behaves strangely in relation to the Hudson. The Appalachians have been an all-powerful dictator in American history. Extending from the St. Lawrence Valley to central Alabama, the line of mountains divides the Atlantic coast from the Mississippi Valley. Even if rivers in the eastern states start out as "tidewaters," in the manner of the Hudson, they soon come to a "fall line" beyond which water rushes down the Appalachian foothills and navigation becomes difficult. But the Hudson, flowing not from the west but almost directly southward, parallels rather than challenges the mountains. To this maneuver the haughty Appalachians are amazingly tolerant. Their offshoot, the Catskills, stop so docilely at the Hudson shore that the river is not deflected. But in one area about twenty-five miles long, known as the Hudson Highlands, the greedy mountains try to interfere by extending into the river's path.

There was an easy way out commonly accepted by even gargantuan rivers. Making a loop eastward, the Hudson could have flowed around the obstruction. But the river was determined to continue in the almost unbroken straight line that is another one of its unusual attributes. It broke its way through the Highlands with what is its narrowest and deepest channel.

How this was achieved is among the mysteries of the Hudson. A cheerful writer, William S. Gerke, had his own theory:

"It is my belief that the Hudson was destined for the Sea as the Sea was for the Hudson. . . . The Sea drove straight to the north as the River was driving straight to the south. Both struck at the heart of the mountains in their path as if impatient for the moment of the meeting of their waters.

"Which was the strongest, the River or the Sea? The River, or so I prefer to think. In the winters, the River hurled its waters filled with grinding ice-floes against the wall. . . . There came a time when the wall was breached, when the River met the outstretched arm of the Sea and they were united at last. Now the tides of the Sea and the flow of the River combined in ceaseless rhythmic movement, in a meeting and mating of their waters. Well, no doubt, geologists will think this the merest romantic drivel. No matter; that is the way I think of it, that is the way it has always seemed to me."

The world traveler, Sir Robert Temple, described the Hudson Highlands "as one of the fairest spectacles to be seen on the earth's surface. Not any other river or strait— not on the Ganges or the Indus, or the Dardanelles, or the Bosphorus, on the Danube or the Rhine, not the Neva or the Nile—have I observed so fairy-like a scene as this on the Hudson. The only water view to rival it is that of the Sea of Marmora, opposite Constantinople."

Washington Irving remembered: "What a time of intense delight was that first sail through the Highlands. I sat on the deck as we slowly tided along at the foot of those stern mountains and gazed with wonder and admiration at the cliffs impending far above me, crowned with forests, with eagles sailing and screaming around them; or beheld rock and tree and sky reflected in the glassy stream. And how solemn and thrilling the scene was as we anchored at night at the foot of these mountains, and everything grew dark and mysterious, and I heard the plaintive note of the whippoorwill, or was startled now and then by the sudden leap and heavy splash of the sturgeon."

At the northern gate of the Highlands, stands its most imposing mountain, Storm King, 1,355 feet high. More than fifty years ago, when I was in my early teens, my mother, in her passion for scenery, bought a summer house imbedded in the opposite declivity, Breakneck Mountain. Our little plateau, several hundred feet above the river, was some hundred yards long and wide, but cosy enough with its crotchety gabled house which Washington Irving would have admired, a large tree, and a miniature barn. A very steep driveway led down to a narrow dirt road (now a numbered highway) along the river. Overhead, the cliff was almost perpendicular, with some saplings hanging on with roots that had probed the rock-like spider's legs.

Breakneck did not feel kindly towards trippers who ignored its name. I was home alone one Saturday morning when there appeared at the door two terribly shaken young men from the city. As they were climbing around above, the footing had given way under a companion, who was lying far below motionless. I sprang on my bicycle and pedaled madly for the local doctor. I have never seen a man less pleased to see me: he was just setting out with his family for a picnic. But the Hippocratic oath is the Hippocratic oath. Having unloaded his family, he set out resentfully in his car. But he was not held for long. The man was dead.

There is often a macabre side to great beauty.

Although the Highlands are acknowledged to be "the gem," there is hardly a reach of the Hudson where the navigated shores and their reflection in the placidly moving waters do not (except where defaced by modern building) excite or charm the eye. Stretching on the west bank, beginning opposite Manhattan and extending north for twenty-five miles, there is an impressive geological oddity. It is as if whatever spirit rules the Appalachians, wishing to restrain his territorial greed, had built himself a high fence that stopped at the very edge of the river's flow. Geologists, who have no belief in ruling spirits, postulate that once upon a time molten lava had poured into a deep crack in the earth where it hardened and remained after the surrounding sandstone had washed away. The cliff, three hundred to five hundred feet high, made up of vertical strata, looks like a gigantic picket fence of rock, thus earning its title, the Palisades.

Near the Palisades's northern end, the river opens up into a miniature ocean called by the Dutch the Tappan Zee, encircled with hills and valleys but now ruined by road builders who found it cheaper to direct the New York Thruway over the shallow water on a hideous viaduct. North of the Tappan Zee in the Highlands, is the only sharp curve in the whole length of the river, the site of the West Point Military Academy. Closer to Albany, the variously peaked Catskill Mountains rise from the west bank.

Its eccentricity in lacking, during all the miles between Albany and the sea, any downward current worthy of consideration made the Hudson the most amenable of rivers. Before the application of steam or gasoline power, it was impractical for boats of any capacity to advance against currents, and there was no practical way to transport bulky goods except by boat. One might assume that, during the generation when the northern end of the Hudson butted wilderness, there had been little need for trade or travel. Yet the most lucrative trade in British America sailed the Hudson's waters.

Furs which could not be produced on the European side

of the Atlantic sold for large prices there. Operating out of Albany, the Dutch inhabitants of New Amsterdam had established a trade alliance with the puissant Indian confederation the Iroquois. Unlike agriculture, which sits comfortably within the boundaries of its fields, the harvesting of furs requires large expanses of forest. Armed by the white man, for generation after generation the Iroquois subjected distant tribes and inflamed the wilderness with mercantile wars against other natives like the Hurons whose partners were the French traders in Canada. Into Albany came a harvest almost worth its weight in gold.

Why, the reader may ask, could not that compact harvest have been carried to the sea coast in canoes? Of course it could. The problem was that the Indians had to be paid. This did not mean pouring gold out of portable money bags. The Indians had no understanding of or use for money. All the more because the fur traders discouraged all Indian activity except hunting and fighting, the tribes had to be completely supported: they were given not only trinkets and guns and ammunition and firewater, but the clothes they wore and almost all their food except the meat brought in by hunters. "Indian truck," the currency of the forests, was bulky, and so were the requirements of the fur traders themselves. Furthermore, as time passed, farmers with their products began (over the opposition of the fur traders) settling in the Mohawk Valley.

In 1807, the Hudson River fostered a new prime mover that was utterly to change the history of the world. As every schoolboy should know, Robert Fulton gave the first really practical demonstration of steam navigation by sending the *Claremont* puffing all the way from New York City to Albany. The Hudson's contributions to this feat were its rigidly controlled waterway—no rolling waves to get machinery off balance—and, since Fulton had not worked out how to build a really powerful engine that would not swamp his boat, no opposing current. As Fulton improved his invention in further vessels and competition appeared, the Hudson, because of its physical peculiarities, remained for years the world capital of steamboat navigation. No boat successfully steamed up the Mississippi until 1817 and the Atlantic was not crossed altogether by steam power until 1838.

Competing for passengers, the owners of the Hudson steamboats overloaded their saloons (public rooms) with such complications of Victorian decoration as were only achievable privately by the very rich. However, the owners had no interest in the local passenger trade, stopping rarely and charging heavily for short runs. Furthermore, their boats were still too crowded with machinery to carry much merchandise. Sailboats remained the normal Hudson River craft.

Although the river argued only with foreseeable tides against the pull of sails, skippers were bedeviled by irrational winds. On open water or in an estuary surrounded with fields, an experienced navigator can trim his sails with assurance, but the Hudson does not go in for tranquil edges. The sailor finds himself in a long, roofless tunnel lined on both shores with irregularly shaped mountains, confused hills, and burrowing valleys from any one of which, when strong winds are blowing, a burst can ricochet at a conceivable angle. If a skipper is not paying the strictest attention, or even if he is, his boat may be endangered in a trice.

Since the human mind prefers the supernatural to the random, the sailboat men attributed the aerial vagaries to Indian curses against the encroaching white man or, more commonly, to mischievous spirits left behind by the Dutch after the British capture of New Amsterdam. Of the resulting folk tales, Washington Irving is the immortal chronicler:

"The captains of the river craft talk of a little bulbous-bottomed Dutch goblin, in trunk hose and sugar-loafed hat, with a speaking trumpet in his hand, which they say keeps the Dunderberg [a mountain below the Highlands]. They declare that they have heard him, in stormy weather, in the midst of turmoil, giving orders in low Dutch, for the piping up of a fresh gust of wind, or the rattling off of another thunder-clap. That sometimes he has been seen surrounded by a crew of little imps, in broad breeches and short doublets, tumbling head over heels in the rack and mist, and playing a thousand gambols in the air, or buzzing like a swarm of flies about Antony's nose [a headland]; and that, at such times, the hurry-scurry of the storm was always greatest. One time a sloop, in passing by the Dunderberg, was overtaken by a thunder-gust, that came scouring round the mountain, and seemed to burst just over the vessel. Though tight and well ballasted, she labored dreadfully, and the water came over the gunwale. All the crew were amazed, when it was discovered that there was a little white sugar-loaf hat on the mast-head, known at once to be the hat of the Heer of the Dunder-

berg. Nobody, however, dared to climb to the mast-head, and get rid of this terrible hat. The sloop continued laboring and rocking, as if she would have rolled her mast overboard, and seemed in continual danger of either upsetting or of running on shore. In this way she drove quite through the Highlands, until she had passed Pollepol's Island, where, it is said, the jurisdiction of the Dunderberg potentate ceases. No sooner had she passed this bourne, than the little hat spun up into the air, like a top, whirled up all the clouds into a vortex, and hurried them back to the summit of the Dunderberg, while the sloop righted herself and sailed on as quietly as if in a millpond. Nothing saved her from utter wreck but the fortunate circumstance of having a horse-shoe nailed against the mast, a wise precaution against evil spirits, since adopted by all the Dutch captains that navigate this haunted river.

"There is another story told of this foul-weather urchin, by Skipper Daniel Ouslesticker, of Fishkill, who was never known to tell a lie. He declared that, in a severe squall, he saw him seated astride of his bowsprit, riding the sloop ashore, full butt against Antony's nose, and that he was exorcised by Dominie Van Gieson, of Esopus, who happened to be on board, and who sang the hymn of St. Nicholas, whereupon the goblin threw himself up in the air like a ball, and went off in a whirlwind, carrying away with him the nightcap of the Dominie's wife, which was discovered the next Sunday morning hanging on the weathercock of Esopus church steeple, at least forty miles off. Several events of this kind having taken place, the regular skippers of the river, for a long time, did not venture to pass the Dunderberg without lowering their peaks, out of homage to the Heer of the mountain, and it was observed that all such as paid this tribute of respect were suffered to pass unmolested."

Geography made the Hudson Valley the most strategic area during the American Revolution. From before the Declaration of Independence until after independence had been officially granted, Manhattan Island served as the main base of the British army, the harbor as the main base of the British fleet. Furthermore, the broad, current-less river, extending all the way from the ocean to the northern wilderness and potentially navigable by the British fleet, presented invaders with the opportunity to divide the rebellion into two separately subduable parts.

Realizing that the only way to win the war with a bang was to drive the enemy from their bases on the lower Hudson, General Washington concocted expedient after expedient, trying to lure his French allies to join with battle plans they always considered crackbrained. And indeed the geographic strength of the fortress defied attack.

Yet solid British control hardly extended beyond the Harlem River, which closed in the top of Manhattan Island. For the next twenty miles or so, the territory east of the Hudson was a no-man's-land, subject to incursions over land and water from either belligerents, and perpetually wracked by the guerrilla warfare that did not exclude robber bands, which is so effectively described by James Fenimore Cooper in his novel *The Spy*. But, except to the tortured inhabitants, this was all small potatoes compared with the strategic issues.

Transportation of supplies across the Hudson was essential to the patriot cause, but the ragged or mountainous hinterland and shoreline made such ferrying feasible only at widely separated crossings. Most convenient was King's Ferry, about twenty-seven miles above Manhattan at Stony Point. This was fortified by the patriots, captured, recaptured, captured again, and finally evacuated by the British when their forces became too engaged elsewhere to hold the intervening territory.

The overwhelming issue was control of the entire navigable river. It first arose in virulent form when Burgoyne marched down from Canada for Albany, presumably to be joined by a powerful army advancing up from Manhattan. The offensive went awry because of confused orders and impractical strategy. The main army in New York City sailed off for Philadelphia, and Burgoyne, unable to keep his supply lines open to Canada through the wild upper Hudson and beyond, surrendered at Saratoga. However, a minor foray from Manhattan revealed that the forts Washington had built to hold closed the Hudson could not resist assault. This resulted in the erection at West Point of the stronger fortifications, expertly designed by the Polish engineer, Thaddeus Kosciusko, that were the major engineering feat of the Continental Army.

During more than three years of hard labor, the soldiers shaped the towering ramparts. Inflated dollars, anguishedly raised, were spent by the millions. The fortification seemed to slant backward as it precipitously mounted the Hudson's west shore. Close to the water, the main redoubt clung to a sheer crag like a monstrous crab. Above, there was a maze-like interweaving of ramparts pierced for cannons. Far overhead, three peaks were topped with semi-independent forts. If you looked downstream, the river seemed to disappear into the hills. This only sharp turn in the entire Hudson River would force any British warship to come almost to a stop under fire from the fortress's cannons. To complete the impediment, a tremendous iron chain was here extended under the river's surface from bank to bank.

As the war was going less and less well for the British, their expeditionary force sinking under its own weight without achieving anything decisive, the Commander-in-Chief, Sir Henry Clinton, became obsessed with the conception of bisecting the rebellion at the Hudson River. But his spies reported that West Point was too strong for capture. Then Clinton's favorite, Major John Andre, whom he had raised beyond ordinary process to the rank of adjutant general, reported that a disgruntled and partially crippled American general was offering to sell his services to the British. Andre advised Benedict Arnold to make use of his disability to secure the stationary post of commandant at West Point, which was a place of merchandise for which His Majesty would pay well. Arnold secured the post. In a sequence of events played out on the Hudson that is unsurpassed for melodrama in all American history, Arnold met with Andre on the banks of the Hudson. The warship to which Andre hoped to return was forced by cannon fire to fall downriver. As he attempted to ride back to Manhattan, Andre was stopped by some of the marauders who haunted no-man's-land. They were probably after his gold watch, but they found incriminating papers in his stockings and turned him over to a patriot post.

The officers there suspected that Arnold was implicated, but felt obliged to follow routine by informing their general of Andre's capture. However, they sent the incriminating documents to Washington, who was on his way to Arnold's headquarters. It was a race to see which messenger would arrive first. Arnold's did so, enabling the traitor to make his escape downriver to the enemy, although Washington, informed only shortly thereafter, sent his aide Alexander Hamilton galloping to try to have him intercepted. But Andre was well caught. To the regret of Washington and all the other American officers the charming young man encountered, he had to be ruled a spy. Andre was hanged at Tappan, in the Hudson Valley, two miles inland from the great river.

Much more significant than Arnold's treason was the crisis—it affected the future of human institutions everywhere—that developed during 1783 in the American encampment at Newburgh, close to the northern gate to the Highlands. As the war was clearly coming to an end, the thirteen states that had joined together to drive out the British turned their attention to establishing their individual independence. Skimping their representation at the Continental Congress, they refused to give that central body funds with which to pay its debts. The two major groups who were being defrauded were the financiers, supporters of the cause who held extensive obligations, and the army, fighters who were owed quantities of back pay. There developed a strong movement, led by Robert Morris and Alexander Hamilton, to have the army impose continental rule on the elected governments of the states.

Here was the beginning of a process that has been repeated again and again in history—it has produced Napoleon, Lenin, Mao Tse-tung, Khomeni, Castro. After a revolution, old institutions have been destroyed and all is chaos. The solution has been to raise a strong man and have him establish order by force. In America, the only possibility for dictator was George Washington. He was offered, in the name of his suffering soldiers, universal power. There are indications that the army was ready and indeed eager to rise. But Washington was immune to the lust for power. At a mass meeting, with great difficulty he persuaded his soldiers to rely on democratic means. Thus was the United States enabled to become, for all the world to see, a beacon light of human freedom.

In its preemptive northward march across the United States, cutting the eastern seaboard off from the central valley, the Appalachian range relaxes only once, in the area of Albany. This break was to have the profoundest effects on the Hudson River and the city at its mouth.

The barrier was of little importance until, after the Revolution, settlers, many of them released veterans, began homesteading beyond the mountains. They found fertile land in abundance, but the great Ohio-Mississippi river system was dominated by a strong downward flow. Produce could be rafted down, but it was a long journey and at the end there was only isolated New Orleans and the Gulf of Mexico. Nothing to speak of could be moved the other way, up the river.

The vast financial and political need of tying the new West with the eastern seaboard by navigable water rather than mountain trails became clearer every year, as did the fact that whichever community was established as the eastern terminus would be immensely profited. George Washington's major activity between the victory

over Britain and the Constitutional Convention was an effort to create at his doorstep in Virginia a Potomac Canal that would climb the Alleghenies in some navigable manner and meet a navigable watercourse on the other side. But geography was too strong even for Washington.

The Hudson River held the cards. Its only major tributary, the Mohawk River, flowed in from the west, and there were a series of minor watercourses that haltingly connected it with Lake Ontario. That the entire system was close to being level with no insurmountable physical impediments opened the way for the Erie Canal. In the third volume of my *History of American Painting*, I thus described the ceremony that marked the joining of the waters of the West with the eastern seaboard and the Atlantic Ocean:

"Governor De Witt Clinton, balancing on the gunwale of a canal-boat, poured water into the Atlantic Ocean from a green and gold keg labeled 'from Lake Erie.' New York Harbor reflected a surrounding circle of frigates, barges bright with banners, and, most exciting to the American imagination, all the fiery spirits that frequented the Hudson River and the Bay. Where else in that November of 1825 could so many steamboats have gathered together as here, where eighteen years before practical mechanical navigation had been born?

" 'The elements,' so poetized the official report, 'seemed to repose as if to gaze on each other and participate in the beauty and grandeur' of what appeared 'more a fair scene than any in which mortals were engaged.' Yet the elements were principals in a surrender as basic to America's future as Cornwallis's at Yorktown. At this opening of the Erie Canal, Distance was handing its sword to Public Works. The East was now linked to the West, and New York City crowned King of the United States."

The Erie Canal revolutionized the economic and social structure of New York City and with it the history of American painting, fostering our first major landscapists, the Hudson River School.

New York City's long established ruling class had their eyes directed across the ocean since their prosperity was largely based on trade with Europe. They had founded the New York Academy of Fine Arts dedicated to elevating American art and taste by the importation of correct aesthetic conceptions. These included the neo-classical belief that the proper study of man was man and that therefore landscape painting, at best an inferior art, became the more unworthy the less the scene had been fashioned by human hands. It followed that the wild banks of the Hudson were not worth painting at all.

Opening to New York City an endlessly prosperous trade with the broad American continent, the Erie Canal created a new class of merchants, usually farmboys who had graduated from behind the counters of country stores, whose eyes turned not to Europe but inland. Uninterested in or ignorant of imported theories, they loved the American landscape in which they had been raised. They were joined in New York City by painters, also self-graduated farmboys, whose views of Hudson River scenery they greatly admired and generously bought. Although the old-fashioned connoisseurs objected, the resulting artistic movement pleased the broad American public which was both nationalistic and romantic; it saw, in depictions of unspoiled nature, a hand much greater than the hands of man—the hand of God. The Hudson River School became the only group of painters in the entire history of America who were admired by a majority of the citizens of the United States. Their works, copiously bought, widely distributed in engravings, and inspiring illustrators of every variety including Currier and Ives, established the Hudson Valley as the capital of American natural beauty.

More modern times have erased the practical importance of many of the Hudson's attributes. The fur trade as early New York knew it is dead. A currentless river or canal can no longer make determining contributions to inland trade. The dictatorial Appalachian mountains have been dethroned as railroads and trucks speed easily through or over them, and airplanes need not notice them at all. Yet what the Hudson basically wrought remains.

West Point, chosen for its geographic location as the best place for closing the Hudson to the British, now houses the United States Military Academy. The government General Washington protected from secession at Newburgh still protects and fosters us all. Modern railways, highways, and airports, continue to pay obeisance to the centers of population and trade erected before their invention. New York City still reigns as America's major center of commerce and culture. Hudson River School paintings, although for several generations eclipsed by new aesthetic importations from Europe and our own development of Abstract Expressionism, have returned to their stature as the most beloved (and among the most valuable) exemplars of American art. And the Hudson Valley still inspires, although in new mediums such as photography, important artistic creators.

This volume celebrates the coming together of the Hudson Valley with a major photographer, Robert Glenn Ketchum. Born in California and raised on the West Coast, Ketchum was lured to the Hudson, so he tells us, because the valley is "a microcosm of the United States in many ways. It is our historical roots, militarily and industrially. Much of the first white civilization grew up on the Hudson shores. We fought for our independence along these same banks." And the Hudson River School painters first established American landscape within the pantheon of world art.

Although Ketchum's photographs have little resemblance in composition—and none, of course, in technique—to Hudson River School landscapes, there is much in his aesthetic approach that resembles that of the painters. In *Letters on Landscape Painting* (1855), the publication which best expressed the doctrines of the Hudson River School, a leading member, Asher B. Durand, wrote that the artist was given "unbounded liberty" by his duty to "perceive in the infinite beauty and significance of nature . . . the time and place where she displays her chief perfections." To find in nature the compositions that best expressed the environment and appealed to their sensibilities, the painters tirelessly explored the Hudson Valley. More than a century later, Ketchum has done the same.

When he selects a conformation that epitomizes for him what he calls "the look" of the Valley, and that beckons to his art, he makes, as he puts it, "the choice" that irrevocably determines the final result. It is now a matter of so positioning the camera as to define the composition he has foreseen, and of selecting the lens, film, and so on that will clothe his vision. Then he must wait

for nature to supply him with the light effects he desires. The release of the camera's shutter then "incorporates the moment."

Durand wrote that when the selection had been effectively made, "the artist will have no occasion to idealize the portrait." Ketchum says the same thing in more modern terms: "Nothing to do in the printing room." He never crops or resorts to any of the techniques that can intervene between the imprint of light on his negative and the finished picture.

In an era of pantheism, Durand saw in landscape the hand of God: "Nature in its wondrous structure and functions is fraught with holy meaning, only surpassed by the light of Revelation." For this reason above all others Nature should not be tampered with. Ketchum said to me that he does not try to improve on Nature because "creation is more sophisticated, complex, and well balanced" than anything man can conceive.

The Hudson River School artists, celebrating symbolically the size of the American continent, often painted extensive vistas. Coming from the far west, where views are so much more extensive than our eastern river can supply, Ketchum has reveled in the tighter landscape of the Hudson. For him, large space dilutes effect. In this one respect of tampering with nature, he uses visual and technical photographic means to shrink distance, thus subscribing to the modern view that a picture, being in actuality two-dimensional, should not violate to a major extent its flatness. This psychologically brings the viewer very close to the image.

Much more than the Hudson River School, Ketchum is concerned with nature in its relationship to man, a necessity dictated by the passage of time. That falls in well with his philosophical conceptions. The primeval forest that the painters found in the recesses of the Catskills is no more, and the valley is crawling with human life. Untamed nature would be, if Ketchum could in his wanderings find an untouched spot, an irrelevant anachronism.

Ketchum's close-ups of nature offer few visible works of man but reveal the imprint of man by showing what results after a time from lumbering or ploughing: thickets of intermingling bush and sapling; meadowlands embellished by the dropping of seeds with a phantasmagoria of shapes and colors. Here is an almost unbelievable richness that Ketchum brings to our view as a revelation.

Speeding through the Hudson Valley at a mile a minute, the typical traveler sees only blurs on the two sides of the highway. Even a stroller would see only what the photographer presents to our sight if he were to stand on one spot staring for a long time without turning his head. In presenting the details the camera records, the artist has found in the scenes he selects designs that sometimes remind us of abstracted impressionist painting. Surely the luxuriance and variety of nature has never been better displayed.

In his more expansive views, Ketchum often shows the homes, industrial sites, and so on that embellish, punctuate, or deface so much of the valley. He has expatiated to me on his concern with having man and nature live harmoniously together. Many of his photographs celebrate such a happy marriage, finding beauty where an ordinary eye would see only the commonplace. The staunch uprights of telegraph poles in their meeting with the thin horizontals of connecting wires, for instance, are

used to give a photograph structure and rhythm. He can make a section of the Taconic Parkway so catch light as to have it cut like a silver scimitar across a dark foreground.

But there are scenes that the photographer, being much concerned with ecology, wishes to propagandize against: dumps of industrial waste, graffiti marring rocks, etc. When I pointed out to him that these photographs too were beautiful, he replied that he had been making a picture: he could not push aside his aesthetic sense. If the picture were not "attractive," he argued, people would not look at it, but beauty can be made "sinister," rather than "appealing, drawing you to look but frightening or repelling you by what you ultimately see."

Although none of the pictures in this volume specifically illustrates the role of the Hudson in bygone years, Ketchum feels that his knowledge and appreciation of the valley's past is present in his photographs because it was part of the sensibility that created his results. Certainly, the illustrations in this book communicate that the part of the world he has recreated with his camera has a deep emotional significance of its own.

In describing his objectives, Ketchum is not afraid to use a word that had been banned as old-fashioned, even Victorian, from much "advanced" art criticism. That word is beauty. Ketchum admits to being afflicted with the passion which John Singleton Copley called "the lust of the eyes." The new vision of beauty Ketchum has imprinted on his plates will remain an important contribution to the Hudson Valley.

Woodlands

This is the land, with milk and honey flowing,
With healing herbs like thistles freely growing,
The place where buds of Aaron's rods are blowing,
O, this is Eden.

Jacob Steendam, *early settler of Manhattan*

December 19, 1983 / 3:30 p.m.

January 8, 1984 / 3:45 p.m.

May 3, 1984 / 12 p.m.

October 30, 1983 / 4:30 p.m.

October 25, 1983 / 3:45 p.m.

April 28, 1984 / 3:45 p.m.

October 24, 1983 / 2:10 p.m.

—Gigantic vast,
O'ershadowing mountains soar, invested thick
Their shaggy waists, and to their summits far
a Wilderness unbounded to the eye,
Profuse, and pathless, unsubdued by toil.
Diminutive beneath, the Hudson, deep
Coerced by rocks, and silent penetrates
The solitudinous and woodland scene;
—struggling for a passage.

John Lambert, *1814*

November 25, 1983 / 4 p.m.

November 29, 1983 / 2 p.m.

November 11, 1983 / 9:15 a.m.

Wetlands

The whole design of the river seems disconcerted. First it runs smoothly, as if meaning to go down the descent as things were ordered; then it angles about and faces the shores; nor are there places wanting where it looks backward, as if unwilling to leave the wilderness, to mingle with the salt! . . . the river fabricates all sorts of images, as if, having broke loose from order, it would try its hand at everything. And yet what does it amount to? After the water has been suffered to have its will, for a time, like a headstrong man, it is gathered together by the hand that made it, and a few rods below you may see it all, flowing on steadily towards the sea, as was foreordained from the first foundation of the "arth!"

James Fenimore Cooper, *The Last of the Mohicans*, 1826

October 8, 1983 / 5:30 p.m.

October 13, 1983 / 12 p.m.

October 11, 1983 / 10 a.m.

November 3, 1983 / 2:15 p.m.

October 13, 1983 / 9:45 a.m.

May 4, 1984 / 2:15 p.m.

October 25, 1983 / 2:45 p.m.

April 24, 1984 / 11:30 a.m.

April 30, 1984 / 2:45 p.m.

Iona is upon the dividing line of temperature. The sea breeze stops here, and its effects are visible upon vegetation. The season is two weeks earlier than at Newburgh, only fourteen miles northward, above the Highlands. It is at the lower entrance to this mountain range. The width of the river between it and Anthony's Nose is only three-eights of a mile— less than at any other point below Albany. The water is deep, and the tidal currents are so swift, that this part of the river is called "The Race."

Benson J. Lossing, 1866

December 20, 1983 / 3:30 p.m.

Meadows

Young Freedom's cannon from these glens
   have thunder'd
And sent their startling echoes o'er the earth;
And not a verdant glade nor mountain hoary
But treasures up within the glorious story.

Charles Fenno Hoffman,
"Moonlight on the Hudson," 1837

October 10, 1983 / 3:30 p.m.

July 11, 1984 / 5:15 p.m.

July 11, 1984 / 2:45 p.m.

November 15, 1983 / 12 p.m.

October 24, 1983 / 3:30 p.m.

December 16, 1983 / 4:30 p.m.

October 21, 1983 / 9 a.m.

History, as we moved Eastward, appeared to meet us, in the look of the land, in its overwrought surface and thicker detail, quite as if she ever consciously declined to cross the border and were aware, precisely of the queer feast we should find in her. The recognition, I profess, was a preposterous ecstasy.

Henry James, *The American Scene*, 1907

October 19, 1983 / 5:45 p.m.

The Highlands and the Parks

What a time of intense delight was that first sail through the Highlands. I sat on the deck as we slowly tided along at the foot of those stern mountains and gazed with wonder and admiration at the cliffs impending far above me, crowned with forests, with eagles sailing and screaming around them; or beheld rock and tree and sky reflected in the glassy stream. And how solemn and thrilling the scene was as we anchored at night at the foot of these mountains, and everything grew dark and mysterious, and I heard the plaintive note of the whippoorwill, or was startled now and then by the sudden leap and heavy splash of the sturgeon.

Washington Irving, *1851*

Bryant Pond Road, Mahopac

The Davis's Boat House at Glenburnie, Lake George, Adirondack Park

Lake Tiorati, Harriman State Park

Along the Trail to the Old Cornish Estate, Highlands State Park

Clove Creek, Cold Spring

The mists were resting on the vale of the Hudson
like drifted snow: tops of distant mountains in the
east were visible—things of another world. The sun
rose from bars of pearly hue . . . . The mist below
the mountain began first to be lighted up, and the
trees on the tops of the lower hills cast their shadows
over the misty surface . . . and the Hudson where
it was uncovered by sight, slept in deep shadow.

Thomas Cole, *1826*

The Cold Spring Chapel

The Vrooman's Pool, Garrison

Tunnel and Tracks, Garrison Station

St. Phillips Episcopalean Church in the Highlands, Garrison

The Russel Wright Home at Manitoga, Garrison

61

(Benedict) Arnold's Flight, Garrison

Upper Lake Cohasset, Harriman State Park

Island Pond, Harriman State Park

Meadow below Lake Tiorati, Harriman State Park

The River

The Hudson is not lordly or majestic. It seems never to change, and it is difficult to avoid the romantic trap of personifying it. The river is beautiful and beguiling, but its survival, unspoiled, now depends to a very large measure on the men who shape its future; they must remain civilized if it is to endure.

John Mylod, 1969

The Popolopen Bridge, Bear Mountain State Park

From the East Shore Looking South and West at Iona Island and Bear Mountain State Park (Panel I)

(Panel II)

The Indian Point Atomic Power Plant from the Eastern Shore, Looking South across the Bay of Peekskill

Railyard adjacent to the Beacon Landing

*Motors skim like swallow over the highways cut on
both banks of the stream in rock faces of the pro-
testing mountains. Long trains pass continually on
either bank; the airplanes soar confidently above all
these. The soft-seeming clouds crown all. It is
enough to thrill the dullest denizen of our old
world. Under the river, on the river, each side of the
river on its near banks, each side of the river on its
high banks, over the river by bridge, above the river
by plane, pass conduit, freight, persons, every conceivable vehicle designed by man. There is perhaps
no other spot in America where so many features,
each remarkable in itself, are grouped . . .*

*If a lama from Thibet or an awakened Patagonian
were to be given, at one wide glance, a vision of
civilization, there is nowhere else to take him than
to the Highlands of the Hudson as now pierced,
crowned and bound with the new works of
twentieth-century man.*

Wallace Nutting, 1927

The Taconic Parkway, North to Albany

The West Shore at Dawn from the Mid-Hudson Bridge, Poughkeepsie

Salt Shed in the Twilight, Ossining

Bear Mountain, Looking South and West from the Garrison Landing

New Hamburg Boat Marina

Storm King in Dawn Light from the Cold Spring Landing

Looking North along the West Shore of Haverstraw Bay

. . . it flows there . . . sliding like time and silence by the vast cliff of the city, girdling the stony isle of life with moving waters—thick with the wastes of earth, dark with our stains, and heavied with our dumpings, rich, rank, beautiful, and unending as all life, all living, as it flows by us, by us, by us, to the sea!

Thomas Wolfe, *Of Time and the River*, 1935

View Northeast from the Osborn Castle, including Garrison, West Point, Constitution Island and World's End, Cold Spring, Storm King, and Newburgh

Afterword

ROBERT GLENN KETCHUM

As a native Californian, I was familiar with a Hudson River that was far more mythological than real. My youth was filled with history books that made the Hudson seem like the center of the world and my more contemporary perspective was further enhanced by the knowledge that New York City was situated at the river's mouth.

My first trips to Manhattan were as a photographer on business and they were also my first exposure to any of the East Coast. It did not seem as the myth had promised. As I stood on a disintegrating pier on the lower west side, staring at New Jersey across a murky, placid, and debris-filled body of water, I wondered. Where were the endless forests of the Revolutionary War that hid our guerilla fighters from the British? Where were the aged buildings that I expected would echo my historical past and give me a sense of my roots as an American? And where was this famous river that served as the principal artery in the founding of the heart of America?

As I discovered, the Hudson is a river and valley that demands more attention if you expect to understand and appreciate it. Its existence is so entwined with history as to insist on some knowledge of that history before you can enjoy the landscape's nuances. The scope of the river and the configurations of the land are not at all like the vigorous Merced or the screaming vertical walls of Yosemite, and yet they are no less grand. The views afforded a traveler are not all-encompassing such as those of the Tetons, but what is revealed from select vantage points does not suffer by any comparison. The American West is more obvious. Everything is right there before your eyes and seemingly bigger than life. But although the Hudson

is born on the side of the tallest moutain in the state and cuts its early course through the Adirondacks—the largest continuous United States park preserve outside of Alaska—this matron of all American rivers is seldom given to hyperbolic displays; her style is demure.

The river and the valley are a lesson in time—time that not only bears meaning to us as antecedents of a history, but time that can be measured by studying the landscape. The essence of the Hudson is what time has wrought. The Adirondacks, the Catskills, and the Highlands that surround the river were all originally vigorous mountains, probably similar in their youthful features to the Sierras and the Rockies. Time changed them, however, wearing them down and making them appear to be something less. The river probably tumbled wildly in its youth, and still does at some of the upper reaches, but for most of its length its broad stillness barely appears to move and seems placid enough to swim across. This proves to be a foolish assumption. Time may have disguised the river's wildness but it has never erased it.

The terrain is swallowed up by the most vast and diverse forest in our country, which basically covers everything east of the Ohio river from the Gulf Coast to the New England border. Beneath the shelter of its canopy, life flourishes. Most of this land was cut over several times in its history, yet aged trees that somehow escaped the woodsman's ax are interspersed with surprising frequency among newer ones, becoming part of a dense skein. This cloak hides the rugged and wilder elements in the landscape. At a distance, the foliage graces all but the sheerest ridges and removes the threatening rock configurations that form a mountain's face. It does not, however, remove the rock lying beneath, which remains as difficult and craggy as ever. Crossing a valley from one ridge to another seems a simple task, but undertaking it is another story. Ravines appear that could not be read in the tree-covered topography. Streams swell them and make many crossings difficult. Rock ledges rise out of the forest floor with no previous hint of their presence and require circumvention. Water cascades everywhere: big falls, little falls, intimate pools, beautiful babbling stretches of a brook, seeping from lichen and moss covered springs, and roaring with force over a myriad of descents. There is so much water that the boggy ground can become impassable.

Even the placid appearance of the Hudson is deceptive. The current is not only powerful; but moves in two directions. The Indians knew. Their name for the Hudson translates as "the river that flows both ways." The ocean's tidal influence causes fluctuations on the river's shoreline of as much as six feet. The incoming course is so strong it delays boats struggling against it and can be felt all the way to Albany, seventy miles upstream from the mouth. After heavy rains the waters are muddy and broiling, awash with logs the size of small boats; and when winter sets in, the river freezes over with its own version of pack ice. Only the largest ships can travel against it, and in the periodic thaws of the season, you can stand on the landings and listen to the groan and creak of the ice plates as they break apart and crash into each other again and again.

Wilderness here is every bit as demanding and unforgiving as it is anywhere else, perhaps even more so because you are lulled by such a gentle profile. Getting lost is easy even if you walk in an area encircled by major highway systems. You could die of exposure while watching the sunset gild the World Trade towers less than fifty miles away. The Hudson and the valley it has carved reveal their wild beauty slowly, subtly unfolding day to day. The miracles of this nature are personal and close at hand. In the same way that the forest comes right into everyone's yard, so do the fleeting moments of wonder and revelation. The most spectacular minutes are just that: minutes when the light is just right after an ice storm and the whole forest seems to be an unfathomable crystal; minutes when a breeze sweeps the trees knocking a thousand fall leaves to the ground in an unimaginable rain of hues; or minutes of realization when overnight a sharp frost changes a hillside you have looked at everyday from a homogenous green wall to a thousand distinct plants, each with its own peculiar shade greeting the change of seasons. This is the secret of the Hudson. The passage of time is the key to enjoying what the valley has to offer because it is in that passing that the river and its environs truly reveal themselves and radiate with their fabled glory.

Initially I spent two fall seasons traveling and camping along the banks of the river trying to absorb what I saw. As an artist, I was interested in the difficulties presented by a subject so rife with calendar-scene picture clichés. I determined that I wanted to approach the river from the perspective of its past and I hoped to find and revisit some of the sights of the important paintings of the Hudson River School. I was not interested in trying to recreate these works, as rephotographic survey projects have done, but rather I wanted to see if those places were still there, and what sort of change, if any, had occurred. When I made pictures at the same location as the Hudson painters, it was incidental. I was not there to copy the past; I was hoping to interpret the change less specifically.

As it developed, the parameters of the project narrowed somewhat, becoming focused on particular areas. Attempting to deal with the entire valley in depth was presumptuous; there was simply too much to comprehend. Although I made images along the whole length of the river, the majority of the work I have done was drawn from the Highlands, an area geologically described by mountainous terrain that rises along the banks of the river, north of Haverstraw on the west side and Peekskill on the east. The flourish of these summits is brief but rugged and ends at Cornwall on the west bank and Beacon on the eastern shore. In the miles between those two points, some very amazing things have occurred and continue to occur.

Once I became involved with a commission to photograph the area, I began to read everything that I could find about the river. I also began to study paintings of the Hudson River School and develop a sense of the specific terrain, so that I would recognize it from the paintings. . The Hudson River School was also of great interest to me because in a previous project I had traced the development of the National Park concept back to early photographers such as Carleton Watkins and William Henry Jackson. Their images influenced legislators that had not seen the wilderness domains of the West, contributing to the passage of the legislation that created the National Parks.

These photographers had borrowed the cause from the Hudson River painters and, in particular, Thomas Cole. Cole loved the Hudson Valley and realized how different it was from the domesticated countrysides of England and Europe. In an address to fellow artists, he suggested that Americans should turn their attention to their own country and paint what they saw rather than emulate the current work being done by Europeans. He felt that the simple rendering of the subject would create a new style, distinguishing emerging American work from everything else being done. He was right. Many other artists heard his argument and joined his ranks, forming a group that has since become known as the Hudson River School, the first school of American art. These men were naturalists and adventurers as well and found great joy exploring the reaches of the valley. Although they traveled widely, especially throughout the new Americas, the core of their work remained centered around the river with its incredible colors, moods, and light. Europeans called their work exaggerated, but American patrons embraced them generously, establishing these painters as the primary artists of the developing culture and allowing their ideology and style to remain unchallenged longer than any other group in the history of American art.

Throughout this period, the industrial revolution swept the land and its demands took a great toll on the valley's natural beauty. Increasing development and pollution began to significantly alter the wilderness environment which had so inspired the Hudson River painters. New demands began to wear away the world they held so dear. For the sake of building New York City, the palisades of the Hudson were being quarried for their brownstone. Much of the game within proximity to any population was hunted out of existence. The abundant fishing began to decline from the combined factors of pollution and overuse. The forests were cut away to build towns and railways and to fuel the homes, ships, and trains. Tracks were laid along either shore all the way from Manhattan to Albany; and mines opened in the Highlands, the Catskills, and the Adirondacks.

The growing population needed a supply source and they took from the land. As their numbers grew, what the land could sustain diminished. The river began to serve as a place to dump their wastes. Remaining woodlands were cleared for ever larger farms and the game retreated even further. Unfortunately for all, the valley had limited resources. Many of these enterprises proved short-lived. Even the farmers became part of the folly when trade with the midwest was opened. This new supply source was so productive it glutted the market. Diminishing the value of products grown in the Hudson, it forced many into bankruptcy. Thus, much had been forsaken for little gain.

No one was more distraught than Thomas Cole, whose pleas for preservation fell on deaf ears. The increasingly prosperous public was caught up in the progress of "manifest destiny" and at that time, the river played too small a part to concern anyone. Yet, Coles's unheeded words may be the building blocks of this country's environmental consciousness, a cause no one had ever previously considered for any location.

The earliest preservation of the Hudson can probably be attributed to the following generation of wealthy in-

dustrialists that prospered from American growth. They, too, appreciated the river's beauty, many of them having grown up on its shores, and they began to relocate their homes outside of Manhattan, building manors not unlike the earlier Dutch. These same families also took a keen interest in the quality of life surrounding their new homes and recognized the destruction being wrought by uncontrolled and careless development. Their concern began a revival of the river. Their commitment is an excellent example for those who are now faced with changes affecting the river's future.

The rock quarrying along the palisades was stopped. Bear Mountain, near the southern entrance to the Highlands, was made a state park and became very popular because one could easily ride a steamer up from Manhattan. In time, the Taconic Parkway and the Bear Mountain Bridge were also constructed to allow a newly mobile public to drive up for a visit. The entire crest of the palisades from New Jersey to Bear Mountain was privately acquired and given to the state as park land. Private property, whether given, purchased, or sometimes taken through condemnation, became the core of what was to be an extensive park system. The Palisades Interstate Park and the Taconic State Park Commissions were created to manage and preserve these areas. When the George Washington Bridge was built connecting Manhattan to the western shore, the Palisades Interstate Parkway was also constructed, linking Bear Mountain to the city along both sides of the river. Soon the acquisition of land in between and around these protected areas began. Additions eventually included Tallman Mt., Blauvelt, Nyack Beach, Rockland, Hook Mountain, High Tor, Stony Point,

Harriman, and the boulder strewn perimeter below the Palisades, now a park bearing that name. Clarence Fahnstock Memorial State Park and the multi-parceled Highlands State Park were added on the eastern shore, all marking an enlightened pattern of concern and balanced use which is resoundingly successful to this day. A recovery had begun. These natural settings are now enjoyed by more people than visit most National Parks. Contemporary additions to this system include parcels intended to complete existent parks and protect controversial lands rescued through the courts, such as Storm King Mountain.

This renewal of preservation was greatly enhanced by scientific progress that began to teach us to appreciate qualities of the river of which initially we were hardly aware. The diversity of life supported by the river's ecosystem was finally assessed and found to be staggering. The river was a major fish spawning ground. It was also one of the principle corridors for migratory birds that traveled the eastern flyway. The great marshes of Iona, Piermont, Constitution, and Tivoli were nesting places for numerous species, and raptors such as eagles hunted the craggy summits of the Highlands and built their eryies in the trees of Iona Island. The tidal flux was perhaps the most amazing element of all for it carried with it warming currents and salt water, creating an extremely complex biology. All the living things that were sustained by the system had adapted to this moderation of temperature and water brackishness brought by the ocean surging up the river. Species from northern forests grew next to succulents and cactuses from warmer southern climes. The Highlands was discovered to be a geological/biological divide between these northern and southern

flora and fauna. In the folds of its mountains and valleys, both zones intermixed prolificly, producing a varietal abundance unmatched anywhere in the United States.

Unfortunately, the news from these scientific discoveries was not all good. The accumulated years of industrial abuse had greatly upset the natural balance, leaving scars and continuing practices that perpetuated many of the river's worst problems. The Albany pool, a still portion of the river right below the city, was, and is, considered to be one of the most toxic water sites ever documented. Industry continued to discharge insufficiently treated waste directly into the river and many of the cities along the river did the same with their sewage because they had never been able to afford complete and proper treatment facilities. Drinking water was drawn directly from the river for some of these very same towns, and lots of people ate fish taken from the river that are potential time bombs to human health, having accumulated tremendous amounts of this toxicity in their edible meat. In spite of its growing network of support, the river began to choke; by the 60's, it was nearly dead.

Fortunately, in the middle of that decade, we seemed to have awakened from a long sleep, not unlike that of Rip Van Winkle. A new environmental consciousness swept the country, and after more than 200 years of abuse, we suddenly realized we were only poisoning ourselves and killing the very things we needed to preserve. With the passage of the Clean Water Act, there was finally some method to attempt the clean up and reclaim what we had lost nationwide; and the Hudson seemed an appropriate place to begin.

Today, the river has partially recovered, but this success will always be a struggle to maintain. Some entities will continue to break the law intentionally, others will try to change the laws for their own benefit. Enforcement depends on current administrations which set the national tone for compliance. Having the most protective regulations in the world and a government that is not committed to enforcing them creates a dangerous situation which encourages potential violators to ignore provisions drafted for the protection of us all and the fragile balance in which we live.

Further threats loom in the future. The ongoing revival of the river poses new problems because rediscovery is bringing increased use. As the popularity of the valley grows, so does its economy and population, placing greater demands on housing, services, and conveniences. What is now farmland, and part of the lasting rural beauty, will be compromised under the pressure of rising real estate values which makes it so financially attractive for owners to sell and subdivide. Increased traffic will warrant cries for the expansion of the highways and the finishing of many country dirt roads. Neighbors will press closer to each other; noise levels will rise; water tables will drop; waste will remain a major management problem. These lingering dilemmas are as yet unresolved. The past has not erased them and the future is only compounding them. Within the confines of the valley, a dramatic confrontation is being acted out as part of a continuing play that is several hundred years old. The characters have all changed many times and each seems to want to alter the set to fit their needs. This ensuing struggle to balance all of these demands is as much our history as is the Revolutionary War. The end result will certainly be as important.

Ultimately, I found the source of the history I had come looking for in the Hudson Valley and I finally could separate it from the myths of Sleepy Hollow and Dutch folklore. Tales may have been conjured up by those living in the valley, but the Hudson was no conjurer's tale nor that of the painters either. The river had far more to teach me than just a rehash of my history lessons. What I really discovered was a microcosm of issues that are national in scope. The name, "Hudson," is interchangeable with hundreds of other locations throughout the country. The problem is not "theirs"; the problem is all of ours—worldwide. Protecting the environment that sustains us is the primary issue of our future and the future of all remaining life on this planet.

If what I have done has any significance, it lies in making us think about these issues. I resolved my initial questions: the Hudson River School and the Luminists really did have light like that; and the autumns, derided by the Europeans as romanticized, were, in fact, more amazing than the painters could render them. But, in retrospect, this information seems ephemeral. During my work, far more important questions arose and we need to resolve those answers before they resolve themselves to our exclusion.

I came away from the valley with the vision of it haunting my thoughts. In that vision there are two versions of the place I have come to love. One is as dark and futureless a location as we will ever know; life there has been cheap and, at this point, the sale has nearly ended. The other vision is of a paradise regained; nothing is cheap and everything is worth far more than its "market" value. My personal choice, and hopefully that reflected by my work, is to struggle and regain that paradise.

ACKNOWLEDGEMENTS

Making these images would have been impossible without the support, help, and hospitality of many individuals and institutions. I would like to thank, first and most importantly, Lila Acheson Wallace, whose generosity provided me with the commission and incentive to spend an extended amount of time in the valley. I am greatly indebted to Barnabas McHenry and the staff at *Reader's Digest* who encouraged me and helped administer the project as it developed.

I have always chosen my camera formats to suit the conditions I encounter. Originally, I hoped to do all of this work with my 4x5. However, the terrain and weather conditions throughout the year were such that at times I could not function adequately with that particular instrument. My problems were resolved by a generous loan from Pentax Corporation of their entire 6cm x 7cm, medium-format camera system with which I ultimately took the majority of pictures.

Much of the land in the Highlands is within the state park system, as is a considerable portion of the western palisade of the river. Access is limited to designated public areas and often seasonally restricted. I am deeply indebted to Director Nash Castro and the Palisades Interstate Park Commission for their cooperation in issuing the permits necessary for my freedom to wander while I worked. The Commission staff and the park police were always there when I had needs or questions and my appreciation for the lands they administer was greatly enhanced by the interest they took in what I was doing.

During the year that I lived in residence in the Highlands, I leased a beautifully restored, two-hundred-year-old home adjacent to Indian Brook. It belonged to Helen and Paul Rosenfeld, and their warmth was reflected in its care. I would like to especially thank them and their neighbors who helped make me feel welcome and often suggested places I should see.

Many of the classic views and prominent overlooks of the river are on private lands, some of which have been estates or farms since the Revolutionary War. Finding these locations and getting permission to visit them repeatedly and with little notice was essential to the success of this effort. Much thanks is due the many willing and interested people I found along the length of the river who, though far too numerous to mention here, were essential to the making of some of my best images.

A few other names deserve specific mention as well. Manitoga and its staff always welcomed me to their lovely preserve. Mrs. Mildred Davis and her son, Jon, invited me to stay at their home on Lake George while I was working in the northern part of the valley. John Serrao, the naturalist at the Greenbrook Sanctuary, amazed me with his knowledge of the flora and fauna, and Don B. Stewart sacrificed an entire fishing season so that I could use his canoe. At Lake Minnewaska I was expertly guided along ski trails by Obiwan, easily the friendliest of all those I met in my travels. The details of my captions and text herein would not be as accurate and complete without the help of Jim Rod, a naturalist with the National Audubon Society; Elizabeth A. Duncker of the Palisades Interstate Park Commission; and author Robert Boyle whose previously published book, *The Hudson River*, weaves together the complex, overall picture of the river.

I would like to thank Ilford, Inc. and its staff who have afforded me assistance over the years with grants of materials. Their Cibachrome paper, which I use exclusively in the printing of all my color work, is the only material I have ever found that made me feel my prints were as good as my transparencies. The great skill in making that happen should be credited to Michael Wilder, my master printer and close friend for over a decade now. His technical expertise and patience makes the lush tonalities of my original prints possible.

I am also honored to have this work released as an Aperture book. For nearly two decades now, Aperture has been one of the primary publishing forces in photography and, as an audience, we are the lucky recipients of their tireless commitment. Michael Hoffman and his staff are dedicated to the vision of this medium and, without them, the history of photography would be considerably less clear. Thank you all for adding my work to this compendium and taking such care to see that my images and ideas are communicated in the most effective way.

Lastly, I would like to thank Carey Ketchum for her advice and encouragement, and most importantly, for being there and sharing it all with me.

ROBERT GLENN KETCHUM